2017
WOMEN'S
MARCH

PROTEST!
March for CHANGE

by Joyce Markovics

T0019811

CHERRY LAKE PRESS

Published in the United States of America by Cherry Lake Publishing Group
Ann Arbor, Michigan
www.cherrylakepublishing.com

Reading Adviser: Marla Conn, MS Ed., Literacy specialist, Read-Ability, Inc.
Content Adviser: Emilye Crosby, PhD
Book Designer: Ed Morgan

Photo Credits: Wikimedia Commons, cover and title page; Wikimedia Commons, 4–5; © Johnny Silvercloud/Shutterstock, 5 top; © Julie Hassett Sutton/Shutterstock, 6 top; © freepik.com, 6 bottom; © BRON/Shutterstock, 7; Wikimedia Commons, 8; Wikimedia Commons, 9 top and bottom; Wikimedia Commons, 10–11; Wikimedia Commons, 11 top; © Evan El-Amin/Shutterstock, 12; © Joseph Sohm/Shutterstock, 13; Wikimedia Commons, 14; © Jamia Wilson, 15 bottom; Courtesy of Library of Congress, 15 top; Wikimedia Commons, 16; Jamia Wilson, 17; © Todd Taulman Photography/Shutterstock, 18 bottom; © Michael Candelori/Shutterstock, 18 top; © Yaacov Dagan/Alamy Stock Photo, 19; © StoopDown/Shutterstock, 21 top; © Sheila Fitzgerald/Shutterstock, 21 bottom.

Cherry Lake Press is an imprint of Cherry Lake Publishing Group.

Library of Congress Cataloging-in-Publication Data

Names: Markovics, Joyce L., author. Title: 2017 women's march / Joyce Markovics.
Description: Ann Arbor : Cherry Lake Publishing, 2021. | Series: Protest!
  march for change | Includes bibliographical references and index. |
  Audience: Grades 2-3
Identifiers: LCCN 2020038481 (print) | LCCN 2020038482 (ebook) | ISBN
  9781534186330 (hardcover) | ISBN 9781534186415 (paperback) | ISBN
  9781534186491 (pdf) | ISBN 9781534186576 (ebook)
Subjects: LCSH: Women's March on Washington (2017)—Juvenile literature. |
  Women's rights—United States—History—21st century—Juvenile
  literature. | Demonstrations—United States—History—21st
  century—Juvenile literature. | Protest movements—United
  States—History—21st century—Juvenile literature. | Human
  rights—United States—History—21st century—Juvenile literature.
Classification: LCC HQ1155 .M37 2021 (print) | LCC HQ1155 (ebook) | DDC
  305.420973—dc23
LC record available at https://lccn.loc.gov/2020038481
LC ebook record available at https://lccn.loc.gov/2020038482

Printed in the United States of America
Corporate Graphics

C⊘NTENTS

HAND IN HAND

A young girl stood smiling between her grandmother and mother. The three generations of females clasped hands. They were among the 5 million people who marched on January 21, 2017. They were **united** by a simple message: women's rights are human rights. "I'm not just doing it for myself . . . I'm doing it for my daughters and granddaughters," shouted a former teacher. People gathered in all 50 states. It was the biggest **protest** in U.S. history!

Of the millions of marchers, many were in Washington, D.C.

That day, people also marched for other issues that relate to women's rights. These included **immigration**, healthcare, and racial **equality**.

Around 500,000 people marched in Washington, D.C. They packed into a large park known as the National Mall. There was a sea of bright-pink hats. People wore them as a symbol of unity and women's rights.

To show their support, women who couldn't join the march knitted pink hats. Then they gave them to the marchers.

Marchers also carried colorful homemade signs. One read "Freedom." Another read "Girl Power!" The protesters sang and chanted "Equality for all" and "The future is female." They marched, side by side, as one big family.

Many men and boys also took part in the march.

WOMEN'S RIGHTS **ARE** HUMAN RIGHTS

I don't care for Trump

RISING UP

Throughout much of U.S. history, women were denied the same rights as men. In the early 1800s, for example, women could not own homes, work at the same jobs as men, or vote.

In 1848, women and their allies gathered in Seneca Falls, New York, to discuss women's rights. The planners created a document that demanded equality for women and the right to vote. Word soon spread around the country. Women began marching and holding rallies. Finally, in 1920, they won voting rights!

The document was called the Declaration of Sentiments.

Lucretia Mott was one of the organizers of the Seneca Falls Convention.

This card was issued for the celebration held at Seneca Falls in 1908 and is added to the roll by Harriot Stanton Blatch

Our Roll of Honor

Containing all the
Signatures to the "Declaration of Sentiments"
Set Forth by the First

Woman's Rights Convention,

held at
Seneca Falls, New York
July 19-20, 1848

LADIES:

Lucretia Mott
Harriet Cady Eaton
Margaret Pryor
Elizabeth Cady Stanton
Eunice Newton Foote
Mary Ann M'Clintock
Margaret Schooley
Martha C. Wright
Jane C. H...

Sophronia Taylor
Cynthia Davis
Hannah Plant
Lucy Jones
Sarah Whitney
Mary H. Hall

Rachel D. Bonnel
Betsey Tewksbury
Rhoda Palmer
Marg...

Even after winning the right to vote, women struggled to be treated fairly and with respect. In the 1960s and 1970s, women started calling for a greater role in society outside the home. They wanted the freedom to choose their own paths, careers, and families. These women called themselves feminists. "We're a movement now," yelled feminist Kate Millett to 50,000 marchers in New York in 1970. Author Betty Friedan led the march. It was known as the Women's Strike for Equality.

The Women's Strike for Equality took place 50 years after women won the right to vote. It celebrated the passing of the 19th Amendment.

In 1963, Betty Friedan wrote a book called *The Feminine Mystique*. It spoke of the need for women to be more than just wives and mothers.

Author and feminist Betty Friedan

Over the next 45 years, women had more choices than ever available to them. But the fight for equal rights is not over. In 2016, Donald Trump, a TV star and businessman, was elected president. He **defeated** Hillary Clinton, even though she had more government experience.

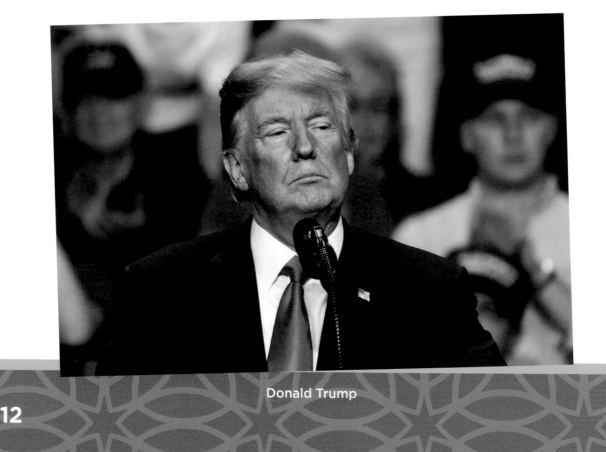

Donald Trump

Trump's election and politics deeply angered many people. He spoke negatively about women—and even about **violating** them. Women and their allies wanted to take action. In response, they planned a march the day after Trump took office.

Hillary Clinton was the most successful female presidential candidate in American history.

The #MeToo movement came to light soon after Trump was elected. That's when many women began speaking out about being **harassed** by men in their workplaces.

THE MARCH

The Women's March took about 3 months to plan. The planners included activists from different races and backgrounds. Each had a unique point of view. As a team, they worked out the details of what would be a massive march. The event was taking shape. Excitement was growing.

The organizers created this poster for the 2017 Women's March.

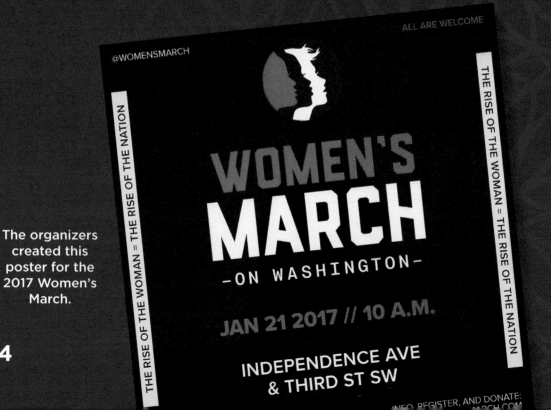

@WOMENSMARCH

ALL ARE WELCOME

THE RISE OF THE WOMAN = THE RISE OF THE NATION

THE RISE OF THE WOMAN = THE RISE OF THE NATION

WOMEN'S MARCH
—ON WASHINGTON—

JAN 21 2017 // 10 A.M.

INDEPENDENCE AVE & THIRD ST SW

INFO, REGISTER, AND DONATE:

Civil rights activists in 1963

Jamia Wilson, a Black woman and feminist, decided that she wanted to be a part of the march. "I come from a long line of activists who 'made a

way out of no way,'" she said. Her family had marched for civil rights and to end segregation.

Jamia Wilson is a writer and feminist in New York City. She's the publisher of *The Feminist Press* at the City University of New York.

"Over the years, I've attended more marches than I can count," said Wilson. "But I knew this one was different when I encountered **droves** of pink-hatted women." The day of the Women's March, people flooded into Washington, D.C. There was an "endless stream of buses," she remembers.

Marchers assembling in Washington, D.C.

Jamia Wilson and filmmaker Alison Fast
at the 2017 Women's March

"We stood together," Wilson said. "When people come together, share resources, and turn our daring discussions into opportunities to grow and change, there's nothing we can't do."

There were 653 separate marches that made up the 2017 Women's March. Organizers expected over 200,000 people to participate in Washington, D.C. Instead, 500,000 showed up!

Different speakers took the stage at the Women's March. They included famous actors and activists. One activist was Gloria Steinem. "Our constitution doesn't begin with 'I, the President,'" she said. "It begins with 'We, the People.'" She went on to say, "We are linked as human beings, not ranked by race or **gender** or class or any other label."

Gloria Steinem is a famous feminist activist.

Sophie Cruz, the youngest speaker that day, was only 6 years old. "Let us fight with love, faith, and courage," she proudly said. "There are still many people who have their hearts filled with love."

Sophie Cruz is a young Mexican American activist. She read her speech in both English and Spanish.

TIME FOR CHANGE

After the march, Hillary Clinton called it "awe-inspiring." Senator Bernie Sanders said Trump should "listen to the needs of women" as well as the needs of all Americans seeking equality. To keep people engaged, the march's organizers called for "10 Actions for the First 100 Days." This included a letter-writing **campaign** and phone calls to senators. The historic 2017 Women's March, with its powerful message of equality for all, **uplifted** and united people. One marcher said, "It changed my attitude. It also changed my action."

Since 2017, other women's marches have taken place. One was in 2018 on the same day as the 2017 march.

TIMELINE

1848

July 19 and 20
The first women's rights convention takes place in Seneca Falls, New York.

1913

March 3
Women march in a parade in Washington, D.C., in support of getting voting rights.

1920

August 18
The 19th Amendment to the U.S. Constitution, giving women the right to vote, becomes law.

1963

February 19
Betty Friedan publishes *The Feminine Mystique*.

1970

August 26
The Women's Strike for Equality march takes place, celebrating the passing of the 19th Amendment.

2016

November 9
Donald Trump defeats Hillary Clinton and wins the presidential election.

2017

January 20
Trump is sworn in as the 45th U.S. president.

January 21
The Women's March takes place.

GLOSSARY

activists (AK-tuh-vists) people who join together to fight for a cause

allies (AL-eyez) friends or supporters

campaign (kam-PAYN) organized action taken in order to achieve a goal

civil rights (SIV-uhl RITES) the rights everyone should have to freedom and equal treatment under the law, regardless of who they are

defeated (dih-FEET-id) beat by someone or something

droves (DROHVZ) large numbers of people

equality (ih-KWAH-lih-tee) the state of being equal, or having the same rights and opportunities as someone else

gender (JEN-dur) the state of being male or female as it relates to society and culture

harassed (huh-RASD) to be bothered by someone again and again

immigration (im-ih-GRAY-shuhn) the action of leaving one's country to live in a new one

protest (PROH-test) an organized public gathering to influence or change something

rallies (RAL-eez) large groups of people coming together to offer support or help for a person or a cause

resources (REE-sors-iz) certain things, such as money or materials, that people need to function

segregation (seg-rih-GAY-shuhn) the practice of separating people by groups, especially by race

united (yoo-NITE-id) joined together for a common purpose

uplifted (uhp-LIFT-id) improved someone's spiritual, social, or intellectual well-being

violating (VYE-uh-layt-ing) assaulting or treating someone disrespectfully

FIND OUT MORE

Books

Henderson, Leah. *Together We March: 25 Protest Movements That Marched into History*. New York: Atheneum Books, 2021.

Hudson, Wade, and Cheryl Willis Hudson, eds. *We Rise, We Resist, We Raise Our Voices*. New York: Crown Books for Young Readers, 2018.

Kluger, Jeffrey. *Raise Your Voice: 12 Protests That Shaped America*. New York: Philomel Books, 2020.

Websites

National Park Service: Women's History—For Kids!
https://www.nps.gov/subjects/womenshistory/for-kids.htm

Smithsonian: Votes for Women
https://www.si.edu/spotlight/votes-for-women

Women's March
https://womensmarch.com

INDEX

ABOUT THE AUTHOR

Joyce Markovics is a writer and history buff. She loves learning about people and telling their stories. This book is dedicated to her friend, Heather, and to all people who march for a more just future.